Bruising Continents

Claudia F. Savage

SPUYTEN DUYVIL
NEW YORK CITY

ACKNOWLEDGEMENTS

Deep gratitude to The Jentel Foundation, Ucross Foundation, and the Atlantic Center for the Arts for the gift of time, space, encouragement, and feeding while this book was written. To the poets of the ACA (Alice Notley, Thandiwe Shiphrah, Ana-Maurine Lara, Jayne Fenton Keane, and Elizabeth Winder) for fueling the ember. My writing group (Stephanie Heit, Joanna Preucel, and Gabrielle Edison) for support and brilliance. And, Jessica C. Dwyer, Ana-Maurine Lara, and Max Regan, for keen eyes and ideas in those early drafts. To tt, of Spuyten Duyvil, for belief in my work. And, my husband and daughter, always.

Gratitude also to the following magazines and anthologies and their editors for publishing poems, sometimes in a slightly different form, in this collection:
Buddhist Poetry Review published page 11 as "Perhaps, Music."
clade song published page 20 as "Alight Before the Sirens."
Columbia Journal published page 27 as "Into Splinters," page 28 as "Into Snow," page 30 as "Into Wind," and page 70 as "Curvature of the Body."
CutBank Literary Magazine published pages 79-86 as "I Will Take the Rain Into My Mouth."
Denver Quarterly published page 64 as "Composition" and pages 37-44 as "Thick in the Throat, Honey."
FRiGG published page 17 as "Into Fire," page 50 as "Folklore II," page 53 as "Rubbing Symmetry," and pages 73-74 as "Folklore I."
Iron Horse Literary Review published page 10 as "Bruising Continents."
Nimrod International Journal published page 47 as "The Limited Visibility of Bees."
She Holds the Face of the World: Ten Years of VoiceCatcher published pages 18-19 as "Thicker Than Water."
VoiceCatcher Journal published pages 18-19 as "Thicker Than Water" and pages 11-12 as "Even in February Every Woman Wants to be a Feast."
Written River published page 5 as "Nantahala."

Epigraphs, in order, from the Robert Hass poem, "August Notebook: A Death," from *The Paris Review*, Winter 2009, No. 191 and Tim Lilburn's, "Marriage and Agriculture," from his book *To the River*.

Additional inspiration and dialogues occurred throughout the writing of this book from the following: Yves Bonnefoy's poem, "The Summer's Night," from *Poems 1959-1975*, translated by Richard Pevear, Alice Notley's *Grave of Light*, Mei-Mei Berssenbrugge's *Nest*, William Carlos Williams' poem, "Asphodel, That Greeny Flower," from *Journey to Love*, Frederico Garcia Lorca's poem, "The Faithless Wife," from *Romancero Gitano*, translated by Stephen Spender and J.L. Gili, Li-Young Lee's poem, "The Waiting," from *The City in Which I Love You*, Pablo Neruda's poem, "III," from *Stones of the Sky*, translated by James Nolan, and Gavin Pretor-Pinney's *The Cloudspotter's Guide: The Science, History, and Culture of Clouds*.

Library of Congress Cataloging-in-Publication Data

Names: Savage, Claudia F. author.
Title: Bruising continents / Claudia F. Savage.
Description: New York City : Spuyten Duyvil, 2016.
Identifiers: LCCN 2016022288 | ISBN 9781944682248
Classification: LCC PS3619.A82875 A6 2016 | DDC 811/.6--dc23
LC record available at https://lccn.loc.gov/2016022288

for John

CONTENTS

. . .build a platform of wood and burn it
In the wind and scatter the ashes in the river.
As if to say, take him, fire, take him, air,
And, river, take him. Downstream. Downstream.

ROBERT HASS

Lay down everything, lay it down.

TIM LILBURN

I

ALIGHT BEFORE THE SIRENS

Once we were river water.

Our murmurings soothed other animals. Cooled
their fevered bodies. They sipped at our banks. Then stayed.

We flowed over rocks as liquid light.
When he first sprouted bone, I reasoned
how small and hollow, bird-like and fit for flying.

I refused to worry.

I sucked at sun. Wild mint made love on my borders.
I flowed. Grasses, dirt. Even mountains.

Bottomless me. Never sufficiently lush.
Around each bend, my current
quickened the length of the moon.

He began to linger. I remember the sound of roots.
The low whine of burrow. My deep harmony
trumpeting, pushing
trumpeting.

And when the stars gathered seductive. Light cold.
We were only connected by dreaming.

Perhaps this is how every bend in a too wide river is made.
One stream seeking forest. The other
longing

　　　　for the quickest path to sea.

Catawba County, N.C.   Icy Coke.   That blue-jeans dress.

I wasn't a precious bird.

His touch made me a seashell with one half eaten. A rare stamp torn.

He said *I love you* easy as *pass the salt.*

He wanted me. He wanted his
feet to my ribs. My arms out.
Legs together (for a moment).

fly

Even in summer. The cells of me suspended fish. Bone
marrowed.

We paddled the warm lake in a dark blue boat. Rib muscles
awake.

Him at the bow. Me behind.

Two strokes right. Two left.
Predictable boat. Even in waves,
wind.

Vivid chemistry of water.
My thighs molten glass.

Should have let him dismantle my tibia tooth
medulla femur follicle gum eye knuckle.
The way his father laid that '72 Olds Cutlass
under the oak when he was 15. *This causes spark.*

His talent at reassembly—
bolt nut puzzle piece puzzle piece.
Even with oil-slicked remainders.
Even with a wire stripped to slim.
In his hands, the dead woke.

At dinner, he looked
for the lost cucumber slice.
Stared hard at my bent middle toe, my weak
right knee, the eyelid that stayed fat
after cortisone. He stored sprockets. Longed
for something to solder after dessert.
My misplaced ventricle would not
whirl unless he helped. Surely.
Surely no meteor shower, no
solar flare would prime my sluggish pump.
Nothing unexpected render the broken un-
broken.

My dress flutters like desert poppies
not yet picked by autumn wind.
          Their petals spread to the sun
like a new mouth.
          His mouth.

It always starts at his mouth.

On the porch I watch the wind push each thought
through his hair, craving altitude.

          Here, in the mountains,
even shadows are blown to rags,
so I should cling to him as it howls.

          The pulse of our years
is in his neck.

The smell of our sheets left too long on the line.

The smell of our bolted garden.

          Early fall, he'll miss the rain,
that younger, dewy us
          opening.

I'll claim to miss nothing.

The sun and I understand
the pleasure of what is brief.
          We bruise the surface of continents,
then turn away.

Zazen in front of the aspen tree.

I am a leaf unhooked.

A forced direction.
I confuse deep water for sky.

    breathe

What did I promise?

Aspen leaves cup sun.
So many months link and release.

If he was here the dappled light
would spot his eyes different kinds
of honey, would make me forget.

We'd lay down. Sleep past its
burning.

I could stop this.

Admit that every bell
is first silent.

It takes a blow
to prove its singing.

Even in February
every woman wants to be a feast.

The year dampness trumped the will of the sun. The year apple trees
he thought barren clung to the last of their fat fruit. The year even

weaker branches had purpose as kindling. That year, he received Jesus.
When the snow reached the window, he sank into the bathtub water

as if he were the source of thaw. Every bird, every cloud, perfect, known.
On the mountain there was no room for confusion, uncertainty, misstep.

He faced the hill to church as mountain goat, even in rain, ice. He bent to the task of
vegetable picking and cotton, though the bag was wider than his slight body.

And when the coffer was empty and his mother cried at the kitchen table,
he offered his saltiest tears to the snow. Optimism feasted on his heart.

He was taught prayers to outlast darkness: *gather*, *save*, *hope*.
Late winter, he lay beside me, searching for the heat off my body.

The snow fell unending. I was a field.
He was not the supple light.

Years of him unwilling. My hips bright grass.

Even metaphor failed us.

BRUISING CONTINENTS

The lit mouth of God ignited the pine. Urged wind to anger. Set creeks boiling.
Rocks to sliver. Deer, raccoons, elk, drowned
in a tidal wave of flame.

Ten years before. September. We bought the old house on a ridgeline.
Smelled the summer air for hints of desperate earth. Stacked firewood
50 feet from the house. Offering.

Late August. We watched the clouds lift from the valley
in the shape of a continent. Red welt bruising blue.
Black bones fissuring unnatural valleys. Aspens unrequited suns.

I wanted to offer him rain.

His arms at my back. Desperate tinder.
Stay murmured into my hair.

Finally, heat from somewhere deep—
pelvis or knees.

Bone sparked bone.

I'll fault his mother. Again.
For years it was *just get mad* at his back, though
I wasn't convincing.

How could I spark the fire
without fearing for the whole forest?

Much later, he told me how she'd howl, *no raised voices, no running*
every time she saw something gleam—
four boys joyous.

It's an old story: they were young. They
could not stop—flames wrapped in skin—
so she wrapped them in silence.

Bitch.

Five years, he would not shout. No chance to bridge our chasm.
Not one fight between us.

       I go.

Like a recent widow all he saw were billowing flames

           tonguing the wind as prayer flags.

All he smelled were a thousand bodies

crushed in heat's anvil.

He forgot there is always another story.   Look

to the seed. A hundred years in soil.

           Its faith in fire. To split the body inside the body.

Burn to color.

Lazarus as name.

He is not even here,
but the dinner is going badly. The guests are talking about evil—
oil and gas drilling, ranching, pork, in such a way that the tone
slants toward that place where country people are only huddling,
dull-eyed sheep bleating for Jesus.

The guest who swirls her Cabernet is delicate in candlelight.
The guest who shivers, doubting the fact that I can shoot, compliments
my green beans. They are forking in the roasted potato, the room.
I want to show the guy my left hook
instead of the apple tart. This
I can stop.

Loving him muddied a line inside me.

I want to tell them, there is a woman in a wheelchair echoing
the blue hills' rain, whether or not I am there to listen.
There is a cabin above the plum orchard
you must stoop to enter. For 130 years its planks
let the world in. At dusk a bluebird's call can carry
through the blackberry to greet twilight.

There is his grandfather trying to save that
man falling into the cement pit, thick dust blinding.
There is his father pushing brooms
through the high school halls to fill his belly.
There is him, hiking into the mountains
in three feet of snow, gusts urging it below 20,
for so many hours that his fingers lose
their sense of touch. Never regain it.
And how he didn't complain as I wrapped quilt
after quilt around him, the skin on his knuckles
elephantine. Cheeks furious with wind.

I want to tell them, no hillside will ever
sigh at your return. No pine sweeten.
His people never trusted me, and now,
have less reason to, still, he made his history mine.

He said this mountain will turn your legs to ghosts. These vines
are good for thickening. He lengthened his vowels
in the curve of my ear till they nested, sun-filled snakes.

Without him, I fear the clay rivers
will not recognize me. I fear there will be no welcoming
hillside, no leaf-tinged light. I fear I will be stuck
hearing Northeasterners chew their fattened beef
at my table forever.

Forgive me. I cocooned in him. A brief place to alight before the sirens.

My wings curled and spotless.
Beside him, I could not feel their longing to turquoise.
The sun inside my throat unaware of its longitude.

I made soup and baked bread. Threw the loose body
upon the hottest stone. Hardened to the task.

When the moon sought his eyelashes, I cupped my
right hand to shelter his dreaming.

Forgive me. I cannot stop imagining
the height of weeds in the garden. The lack
of winter meals. So much gathered, then flung away.

If asked, I would have stayed his Sisyphus.
Always the mountains, darling, and someone unable.

Burden me, till I'm remembered butterfly.

II

CIRCADIAN

Dark, warm water.

I float.

That echo in my ears.
What the night
sweetens itself with. Long moan
of a fattened river. Heavy clouds
greet thunder.

In the midst of green.
Floating soft and small.

The canopy inhales.

It makes no sense. I dive the water
searching for fire. One match against
the placid ink.

Burning, I swim hard towards
the ripened fruit. Shake the branch. Cause
another fall.

Late morning. The same trail for continuity.

A rivulet of sun through my favorite pine—the one tested
for pygmy owls—two short raps to its desiccated heart.

My torso harbors something winged. It doesn't tire.

I walk my succulent ankles to spears. Trees
shed the extraneous.

Beg for spring. I plead with winter.
Smother my brightest leaves.

Turn me vapor.

Make me a scarlet berry on a dormant tree.

No. Better. Make me a downed bird pierced by the branch
it called home. Widen the wound and wonder at my heart's color.

While there, eat my lungs. Lick my spine pale.
Till nothing weights my vertebrae.

I'll contrast air with air.

Snow is more lovely under night's wing. Lips
after pressure's kiss.

If you must. Clear-cut winter's trees.
Flood the remainder.

Wild birds flee my shadow. I stroke the neck's bowl. Each pore a starfish soaked with sea.

Cattails heed the call of winter. Flush to rubies.

And sun ambers the room. Through the window, a cold breeze brings him. As pillager. Knife on a flexed thigh. Him. As whatever fantasy worked when he stopped wanting.

I will not open my eyes until he leaves. This is not.
His name on my finger's tip. Not. His body. Improbable stir. Flush. Flood.
My oasis. Here. Oasis mine.

Only granite could bookend
my star-flung shadow.

That night, I walked the steepest face by moon.

The wind ripped at my eyes, so I shut them
to claim old names—Tiresias, Inanna.

Consonants off the pebbles of my teeth.

Almost there, a turquoise butterfly's wing
beneath my foot, locked in snow.

Not now, I thought, but picked it anyway.

In the dark universe of my left palm it thawed. With heat,
it trembled. *I'll call you beauty*.

The wind wouldn't get everything.

I would be the sea. The color
of new eyes.

Bear down without froth. Without
fury.

I would stop. So sick
of how we grow thirstier.

Oh, to be a winter tree
when the sap slows.

Bittersweet
shiver. Unquiet this life.

Unbelievable.
The first time alone in thirteen years.
I dream of him.

He carries my rocking chair. Places it
by the southeast window. The one
that ushers early light.

Sun-filled eyebrows. Arms
braided tongues of muscle.
Beauty's halo strong.

Often, on the cusp of sleep, he would brush my hair
from my forehead. (Imagine his palm as shield.)
To think of me alone—even when dreaming—
impossible. My penchant for turning wild grass.
Being lost. And he could never get there.
To wield daggers. Play samurai.

Worse.
I never looked for him.

Tonight my sleeping-self lingers
as he sets woolen cushions.

I beg my mind
to slow the changing colors.
Ignore the binding covers.
The bladder's desperation. Until it's useless.
The chair is daisies. The window horizon.
The cushions air. Once again,
I'm gone.

III

THICK IN THE THROAT, HONEY

I'll blame it on the jungle.   The bees knew.   Their wings heavy
     through the soupy air. That constant sound of armadillos snuffling the dead leaves
long tongues poking for treasure.

I hated heat until that month.

     I'll blame it on the lizard that got lost in my room and pulsed its giant
red throat   when I cupped it in my hand.

Everything was a heartbeat.

     I'll blame it on the night you asked me to walk the bamboo bridges
     above the canopy.   Dared me to stare at three-foot spider webs in lamplight.
That month nothing scared me.   Not   the giant spiders full of fur.   Not
the alligators swimming beside our rooms.   Not   the fire ants that ravaged my toes.

I was the flame.

     The webs   harbingers of moonlight   intricate stars.
Intricate pattern of my heart.   You found me and wove music through my hair.

     Six days the Everglades burned.   We might have made that persimmon moon.
     Fat round joy.   Into the lantern-lit ocean.   Sparked once more.
Once more.

                              Thick in the throat, honey.

You ask me to take off my shirt.

          Your eyes smooth lakes
       to paddle through. Even before you reach for me, I know

I will refuse you
nothing.

                    In the still, gray light
                    you trace
                    my hemispheres.

I'm loose sugar.
Sweet-scattered
under your fingers'
oscillation.

Give me back.

Give me back
to the dawn.

You made me your
pale autumn thing,
curved at the neck
as if weeping.

You made me your
broken fast, a feast
unending.

I want to blame me.

I shivered at your gaze, and
what man could refuse
such obeisance?

Possibly, I should've
accepted my beauty.
Sadness can work us,
sand to pearl.

That year, alone
in my one room,
I worried my choice
to leave him.

Thirteen years. My
adult life reduced to
mere memory.

After that
it didn't matter
who parted the sea.

I should've said,
Here is your treasure.
Open me.

If winter nested
in your ribs how did I
sway you
    toward the first iris—
    shudder the air abloom?

            was it simply
    you
    as dry field
        me
        the thawed river? All
I remember was the way

day three
made we—the oasis of our mouths
    the day's heat off your neck
    waxing crescents
        of unwrapped skin.

We make our own myths:

His touch echoed dawn.
Entering her torched the Everglades.

We could never go home again.

IMMOLATE

Hafiz was right.
     There are those of us who want too much.
Our hearts bruising the small ribs given.
We look into the eyes of someone on the street
and want to break their mouths with our breath.

I sit on my porch and wish for you, a man I barely know.
     I want to be ashamed of these thoughts,
but I just pulse with the bees
that have invaded the roof
of my neighbor's house.

They dance ecstatically in the morning light,
their persuasive song straining their undersized container.

     The queen has set them on fire.

How I long to be her, deep inside an eave, my message
     so clear it tinders the cool air to flame:

take me
take me
come
take me
on

Give my hair to the wind.

Light my feet with fallen wood.

I am ready

for the cries that come

from loosened spine.

For the clavicle to be vessel   cup   bowl.

I welcome you, smell of lit hay. Sweetness in my lungs.

Sun   no sun.
Cloud   no cloud.

No matter.

Devour my mouth.

July.   The garden submits.
Color leached.

Afternoon clouds fevered to mob.
Our fevered throats.

Twelve more days.
Until you.

Last night your voice turned me
dense forest.

Are trees terrified of lightning?
I have not slept.   Waiting.

More resilient, more beautiful.
Promise me.

Unaware I was thunderstorm
the first touch leaves you rhapsodic.

Soon we're comparing longitudes:
hip to calf, stomach to heart,
finger pushing for rib bone,
capricious clouds
rejoining the mouth's river.

To love long-distance is to
worry the birds
for twelve-hundred miles,
over the Rockies, the Cascades,
bits of blood,
skin, polluting the snow,
choking the sea.

We thought we could stop. Find someone
nice in our own cities.

But then you are off the plane.
Your mouth rain-filled wood.
Smoked tea in your hair. Your eyes.
Your eyes.

It seems simple.

The fire rises in you.
I am effervescent.

Long cool drink of water.

Deep pool where the sharks hunt.

Crushed indigo.

How will I keep you burning

when I lack weathervane

and there is no guarantee of lightning

no collision of heat?

I ask you to look deeper

at the singed trees

along my spine.

To not be distracted

by my shoulders' healthy pine.

To let your lips maroon when I pull my hair

up

let slip

the tender skin

that has never felt the sun.

Watch as you cross a room.

    You cross

                      a room.

To tongue that bright spot.

Hungry match.   Thirsty wood.

In the dark   we might.

The same three feet   for hours.

If I were a painter, I would charcoal
each freckle, each mole. Slow.

Both crave   and refuse light.

Back to chest we stand over the bathroom sink.
Your chin on my head. My color returns—
toffee, tinged with emeralds. Above me, you burn
lit pomegranate.

Is there a candle   I can't remember.

You lead me to the still damp sheets. Shiver.
Shiver. Before we

comet the night.

Not far north flames gallop
the ridgeline, the season manifest.
You grasp my armpits in the warm spring
stretch my torso loose
till the hips unfold   as ripe figs.

Raindrops shimmer water between us
your breath an echo of its trembling while
the trees sing us into a summer night so dark
my nipples turn   scarlet wine, instead of steeped tea.

The fire between us, for a moment, blind ripples
like that last note of Schumann you will play me later
almost inaudible, rising with our heat to the ceiling, spreading
so gentle, so prolonged   I am unsure when it might fall.

Pet names soothe, so I call you *baby* and *darling*
though I'm desperate for the familiar timbre of my name across the sheets.
The consonants softened by generations of mountain people. The mossy vowels
and last syllable swallowed by the creek rising.

No place ever creased my dry skin with its dirt.
I longed for a man who knew which wild leaves edible. Which fruits jam easiest.
How to stew any flesh.

Strange to cross a continent for another equally clothed by rain
and damp earth. Grandparents who measured the year by seed and dearth
of light. Another whose childhood lack made each woman's touch a dawn
of shooting stars.

These are things I do not say:

Your eyes startle me that first morning, sea instead of sun-
tipped wheat. I cannot help contrasting one, wide and
thickly muscled, awkward at the task of my body, the other
long, soft, hands purposeful and sure…

wheat   sea

wheat   sea

sorrow

sorrow

Two days of lovemaking.

Scent-soaked. You leave
in the dark. It takes hours for the air
to contract. No one believes it, but I
abandon the sun. Sleep through that first
wave of loneliness. Call it exhaustion,
since it feels too soon for need. 1911
apartment aftermath. My friends think
malevolent Methodist ghosts will turn on
the gas in the middle of the night. Will crank
the shower. Drown me in steam. They can't know
the mattress offers refuge to every hair and eyelash.
Later. In the stilled dark. Only your satisfied bellow
oozes from the walls as glue. My eyes, my hands,
wake desperate for anything resembling your body.
Is it too early to call, to beg? What would I say?
Even a continent away, I want.

I fear you.

Your hips

the only worthy summit
my tongue crests
the left one rapidly to
ignite your eyes to
feral the soft daggers
of your mane to
release your spine sweat free.

Late afternoon is hardest.

Maple leaves cave to light's indecision

and the wind promises

your voice.

Your neck.

You.

Damn you.

I'm summer-stripped.

Try undulating thoughts.

Get undulating sky.

Picture thighs as broad roots. Hair, a canopy deepening.
Unfolding from chair to ceiling (think) healthy tree.

My back prepared to nestle your longest limb. Vertebrae by vertebrae.
Nights as sated cat. Your leaves gifting breezes through the arched tunnel of pressed paws.

Snowy springs would gather in your arms' expanse.
Lightning seek weaker ground.

Fall in Colorado spiteful. Never enough blankets. Even the moon withholding.
I dove into you.

Occupation by other beasts dismissed. None could have ravaged your base in four years.
(Think of her as termite.)

None could have hollowed your sides in eight.
(Think of her as woodpecker.)

Whatever.
You'd hold.

You'd hold.
I would be your lone, obsessed companion.

Darkening night.
My false leap.

Falling, my eyes.
My God,

sky

And, you? Hundreds of miles away.
Those unbearably long arms. Ghosts under my back.
Binding fragments of me.

You no longer deserve
to be my muse.

Shifting the clouds with your thumb.
I know wind surfs the seashelled valleys
of your ear. That gaping hole of mouth
sucks every last bit of oxygen
from the trees.

You saw I could be rain.
I'll never forgive you.

Don't make me admit
in a ruined city
I would still
call out, pinned under rubble,
for you.

The rain wants to be music.

Improvise gravel. Blossom circles. Move
to move. Vibrate joy.

The pine needles desire to be splendid.

Drops perched light. For each finger. Tension held.
They illuminate the forest. Slick russet bark
made more russet in their glow.

I wear no hat.

My ears freeze. My thighs numb. Grass below me gray-green
and sparkling. The rain keeps its tempo. Down my forehead.
Over my nose. My chin slick with it.

I remember the young man who drove to kiss me every time it rained.

The iron clouds. His hot mouth. My hot mouth.
Stomach warmed to gold.

I remember you moved from forest to city. Standing outside when it rained.
The drumming in you like too near thunder. I know your lips
worried the water of your mouth.

I can hardly stand.

Through the mist. Soft ground yields. I think *give*.
And you are here.
Open.

I admit to wanting the fire's ruin   as much as its light.

Everything is a gift.   The clouds draw and pull as jellyfish

    in a troubled sea.   I wait for the rumble.

For the hair on my neck to rise to it.

I am drawn to heat to prove   I can stand my fear.

Don't say caution.   I know your mouth.

Tongue a lightning bolt.   Fellow marrow sucker, your lips

    could crack open   the roof of the world.

You should say, *break the horse of uncertainty and the spirit goes, too*. You should know I'm greedy. I'll divide, then build on predictability. I'll take your lower lip, its shelf swollen for the upper's outstretched wings. And the smooth warmth of your elbow joint as it awakens to my ribs' weight. But, then, his forearms, bulbous gourds of blood. His back pushing two shoulder sockets to the edge of his body's map as he lifts the dog, a mile to go, when her paws were full of cactus. It wasn't just that he did it, it was how, cooing, *it's OK, baby*, into her left ear and how her body went limp in his arms, her head falling to his ministrations. Still, I can't see how your bright spirit, a lantern of sea urchin, will fit into his tortoise shell. Or how his heartbeat, thickened by years of restraint, can be staccatoed.

I'm still not certain how to build a man.

SUGAR

My body lay fallow   seven years

a vise of shuddering burrs encircling my length.
      Each wind enough
            to set dry brush to flame.

Spring after spring the hills behind our house   shamed me

with their sky-mirrored
      flax. Their wild daises. Their
            seed heads tipped with light.

Even in drought   one lush rain
      and pale sand
            ripened to black cake.

Beside him I pulled the clover and thistle.   My back was strong.
      Sometimes
            the work spoke for us.

Sometimes the hills mocked us with their perfect   greening.

You saw underneath my untended skin
      rich earth
            resting.

You brought me strawberry vines   so late in summer
      persuaded tendrils
            to breach fat and bone.

I could lie, *he was always cruel.*   But it is simple.
      You brought me berries.

           I claimed sugar.

Quick.   Forget.

Insert vowel for consonant.
You becomes he, though he could never be that.

On the phone it is hard to say his name.
I want to shorten him to a letter.
Something easily expelled.
We are talking about the dog
or who gets the leopard chair.

I'm desperate to use forbidden words.

Stuck in my throat: *dear*. Coating teeth: *honey*.
Hostage behind ribs: *my love*.

I did it. My choice to leave. I thought
I'd fastened the night. But he turned
new moon. Invisible to all but thick
in the dark of me.

Once. The tributaries of me rose to be named by his hands. Hands
beaten by cold's variance. Dried. Thick and desperate.   Even so.

Now. From the west. Rain.

We are never truly sated
        even when we shed this day   pressing what's cool
                against what's eager.

Warmth rises up   as sun defies the night.

Ravenous after a swim in the river we fall
        on our tuna sandwiches.
                Our mossy toes raw silk.

I worry that bellies now full turn hollow.   Clouds bind light.

You sigh onto the warmest patch of rock
        lick my shoulder's sorrow. Stroke my back as cartographer.
                Make me mouth *again* again.

The world is filled with too much light and I can't see the stars
and dear God where are you when I turn away?

The world is filled with too much time to think about
where we should go next. Who we should be next. And
next is too soon too soon.

Begin again.

The world is filled with you.

It would be you first. My knees supple and your beard
unstreaked. It would be me in Berlin stealing your spätzle.
Me with a tick in Austria. Me hollering in the jazz club in Mexico.

It would be you waiting in line outside the Louvre.
You phoning me in Prague. Us waiting out the rain
in the Blue Ridge Mountains in a tiny tent.

At 20, my mother gave paintings as payment in the English
countryside. Someone left the gate open. A pitcher at the
spring for anyone to take a drink. A sheep wandered. Its lips
velvet against her dandelion-offering palm.

See her strolling in that fitted wool skirt.
Her waist the circumference of a yawn.

If I could do it again, she said, I would've run off with my
friend's cousin. Eyes so green against that smoky hair. His
emerald sweaters. Kissing against the stairwell before dinner.
London accent. Proper enunciation for improper places.

Afterwards. The pictures of her afterwards.
Shoulders bare. Collarbones sharpened wings.

In your arms my body melts into unknown shapes. We
improvise patterns. How I get to work I never know.

In the morning music waits in your hair.
A hum tucked in cheek.

When I return in the evening your flute sounds thick.
Wooden. When I reach the third floor it transforms
to gold. A rose. Pennies in vinegar. Floating.

The room tells my fortune.
My life will be deep, deep breath.

Right in the middle.
If there could be a middle.
While you are in the middle of me.

Right.   This is just how we started

you finding the true length
of those fingers, and, good lord,
it feels just as wild, just as
hallelujah, as it was then.

In fact.   It might be better

might be, if possible, better,
because, we almost missed this.

Your tangy tongue.   Thought I wouldn't

want it Wednesday, Thursday, Friday,
Tuesday, every day, this is just what I,
just what we, need before dinner, bed,
work, this moment with you.

Thought I would live.   Near the river's heart

frozen waterfalls of mud, cruel wind,
no way down the highway in winter, you said,
closed down, shut out, sequestered,
and I told you, *I once lived at the mountain's whim,*
I can handle an hour away,
but, *I can't,* you said, *I can't.*

In spring.   When flowers dilate

petals, it is just an extension
of every other season, just a
different shade of green, gooey,

moldy, budding, can't believe
it never stops, never stops, there is no
winter, but really, don't you just
love the rain, the way mist clings to the evergreens
like a cloak of love, some would say
it is easier, the wall of water sideways,
the gray linger, but snow, remember to
miss me, now that I'm gone.

In the east.   My sister trembles

under a thousand blankets, a friend gifts me
an autumnal crocus, already it flowers though
it is only February, for a year it can feed itself,
eat its own insides, for a year sustained, I was
like that once, not needing soil, tending, for a year
no one noticed if I passed out from fever,
if I didn't show up, get up, straight up, I'll
take it once more, no one cares.

Now.   I have your

beard of fox fur, gray, red, silver, blonde,
your chin blended prairie, I'm smitten, an overfed
kitten in your bed, in one story, you are ice
and I am snow, in this one, we are both molten,
careening into clouds, both unstoppable, even
in this dark bed, through the rain, burning.

CODA

FOLKLORE

I will take the rain into my mouth

as if it were your skin
complicit, I can be a pleasure-bird
seeking the damp seed
the well-oiled wing
in the corner of what explodes

quickly, so as not to wake the evening

I will weave mist into my hair
as if I bore it
clouds unblue
tuck into
dreams of
sapphire

sunsets
cough red
orange scream
stars alerted to
their queen

when I wade into the Willamette
the barren trees my bridesmaids
the fog my coat
the fields hush
the highways

for roses to unfurl
sodden scent
blighted leaf
a second time
pale, weeping figs
colored as grass
protect their flower

rosemary thickens wild
persimmons wash
the muted
heavens

~

we sleep past the lit wood and poured tea

a sigh against my shoulder
holds that dappled light

cinnamon in my hair
your neck exposing
its honey

my pale finger
startled snow
against the sheet
glow hazy
breasts below
a day-spied
moon

when we greet the rain, you seek the soggy roots

the maiden hair and fir
stomped through this
dark grey lullaby of
beaten maple
triumphant spruce

~

the salmon might make me an optimist

returning

hook-nosed and wonder-eyed
giant silver fish, dinosaur fish
braver than us
sacrificing fish, returning
a blanket of troubled river hushes
the waterfall
where they leapt 14,000 years
still it seeps, weeps
magic water falls and
falls

as berry leaves, as ivy crowds the corners
of my head
and the city floods
and a thousand beers a night
pour
and a thousand coffees a day
pour
and movies sell out
and pork belly's in

every breakfast
noodle swirl
ice cream bowl
and bike fenders sing
and scarves squeeze
and the feral ring-tailed cat
I covet
hard curls
my front door

softly, I will court the sun

confide in the crocus
the solution to our malaise:
rain, rain,
down the drain, drain

I'll sacrifice your yard chicken

offer my naked sight
to the frightened light

~

the key to the Pacific Northwest is a wool hat and good jacket:

whiskey helps
coffee helps
fucking helps

sometimes

~

there is deeper quiet somewhere when
we escape further west
the churning Pacific wind scoops at
my brain like butter and I'm
lost to the rocks
as foam
as seagull
as crab feast
by sandpiper
needing
soft meat
sweet sweet

the sun must agree

to end my misery
wind threatens
the bone-pulsed
hemlocks with
permanent gale
we stop looking for
whole sand dollars
bare feet
to the icy water
kelp kite at my toe
giant clams suck the roof
for air

~

if I say yes to you

your city, fate, yes

will the volcanoes dream
their worried dreams
the Columbia remember
a time before steel
the blackberry thicket's ardor

when I fly into strange and dark
salty grasses, nights on fire
hidden fish glowing at the muscle
will you follow
to a place where you can throw your lungs
into that horn
and the herbs sacrifice their young
to a god of your making

~

sun after days upon nights upon days of water
I warm your mouth with my mouth

we vibrate the air

once more

CLAUDIA F. SAVAGE is one-half of the improvising performance duo Thick in the Throat, Honey and co-runs the music-poetry label Thrum Recordings. Her poems, essays, and interviews have been in Water-Stone Review, Denver Quarterly, Columbia, BOMB, clade song, Late Night Library, Bookslut, Nimrod, Forklift, Ohio, and elsewhere. Her series, "Witness the Hour: Conversations with Arab-American Poets Across the Diaspora," is a 2016-17 feature in Drunken Boat. She has been a Pushcart and Best New Poets nominee. Her collaboration, reductions, about motherhood and ephemerality, with Detroit visual artist Jacklyn Brickman, is forthcoming. She's garnered awards from Jentel, Ucross, The Atlantic Center for the Arts, and Portland's Regional Arts and Culture Council. She lives with her husband and daughter in Portland, Oregon. *Bruising Continents* is her first collection.

claudiafsavage.com

40292001R00063

Made in the USA
Middletown, DE
08 February 2017